ADVANCE PRAISE FOR

Before the Fevered Snow

When I read Megan Merchant's poems, I'm left breathless. They are almost too much to bear, and I ask myself, "how does she sustain this level of intensity, line after line?" In her latest collection, *Before the Fevered Snow*, Merchant invites—demands—us to enter through "dark doorways" where crows, owls, bones, and spiders litter the "bluetiful" American landscape. This is a fraught place, strewn with guns and horses, bound by "the thick tissue of motherhood," and, like most things American, elegiac. Merchant's examination of grief and joy within this world, where "even beauty is surrounded by hard," is precise and gorgeous as a "violin balancing on a raven's back." The loss of a mother, the ache of marriage, the burden of mothering are woven into a tapestry depicting a world that squeezes the heart "three times." I will visit the indigo and bone places in *Before the Fevered Snow* again and again, because they are "so damn beautiful."

JENNIFER MARTELLI,
Author of *The Uncanny Valley* and *My Tarantella*

Megan Merchant's poetry has the sudden fall into dream, tenderness, awakenings and delicate and crystalline images—the tone and lines are just right and seem to be in the language of a forest at night and the unseen eye in the wave.

JUAN FELIPE HERRERA
2017 U.S. Poet Laureate & author of *Everyday We Get More Illegal*

Before the Fevered Snow uses precise metaphorical leaps to weave its verbal nesting of autism, dementia, depression and parenting, and love despite the losses, with images of birds and bone and winter. This is a book of caretaking against grief. Megan Merchant draws her poems chiaroscuro with shadow and light, caught like Eurydice between the passing things of this world, where a crow's "feathers make dark doorways in the snow." We walk through those doorways with her, in tight lyric poems—most no more than a single page—so we can keep living, so we can keep giving, even "after the last wound is sewn," even after "my body became this bowl."

SEAN THOMAS DOUGHERTY
Author of *The Second O of Sorrow*

Before the Fevered Snow

MEGAN MERCHANT

STILL
HOUSE
PRESS

FAIRFAX, VIRGINIA

Stillhouse Press
4400 University Drive, 3E4
Fairfax, VA 22030
www.stillhousepress.org

Stillhouse Press is an independent, student-run nonprofit press based out of Northern
Virginia and established in collaboration with the Fall for the Book festival.

Library of Congress Control Number: 2019920369
ISBN-13: 978-0-9969816-5-1

Designed and composed by Douglas Luman.

I

Boneyard

I watched the winged seeds slip from the maple,
and for a glance—fly.

This coming of winter. I tried to believe the world
wants us to break even.

But mint and wool. But horsehair and cinnamon.
But bones and silk.

Last night, a pack of coyotes chewed a raven until
black feathers blessed the ground.

I watched a woman walk into that dark acre
with a spear. As if she could nick

the heart of what hunts us. And her leathers would
keep teeth from breaking the skin.

I cannot remember the last time I looked at a stranger
and wanted to know how

they might kiss. If their mouth tastes of the unsaid.
If the coyotes, after gnawing blood,

are able to sing a new song. If the twisted branch,
emptied of leaves

for the first time in months, can hold
such delicate weight.

Hollow

The hummingbird mum sits on her babies
in the morning frost. There is the smell of smoke—

someone else's warmth thinning to reach me.

I hang sugar-water from a red string, the plastic
flowers, loud yellow—always in bloom.

My husband, on the porch, fiddles with a banjo,
giving his hands something to cradle, to yowl.

He plays a fringe of nerves firing, like spring.

I sink my skin into a bath of fennel,
swallow enough that it might become a small

pit in my belly. A root. For feathers,
I chew a single strand of hair.

Nesting

I visit their growth before the light
wades into the tree-line and warms the nest.

The cold dew grips the spider silk that threads
the cup of leaf-litter and twig.

In this wild, I have the privilege of speaking softly,
letting my shadow and footfalls groove a path

so that I can find them in the thicket, again,
past the flooding creek bed, weed-sprout and stone.

They have grown easy with my presence.
They have grown.

My mother, asleep under a weighted blanket,
is slipping farther into the dark. Her brain stuttering memories.

It is spring, but we are still wintering a garden of shapes and colors.
Re-learning words to name her wants—

rusted hinges to the doors she needs open to feel safe.

When she wakes in a panic, I try to hush the flailing.
Wrap her close. Both wing and arm, trying to get a hold of the air.

I Will Explain

The black cat she named
after a stiff Russian drink,

and that slept on my childhood
bed, crawls out from under some

orbit—neither of us can remember
the exact shade of red lipstick

she was always wiping clean.

//

If given the gift of another question
I would choose one that could
unpack like nesting dolls.

//

I would ask again about my birth
story, how I almost arrived

in a donut shop, how a city
bus driver stopped and picked
her up, going off route to the hospital.

It feels important to plant this here.
The hospice workers say only hours might

be left. Nobody knows for sure.

//

I read that I was an egg in her body,
when she was tucked and growing

in her mother. That to find my true
age, I'm to subtract 20 weeks
from the moment of her birth.

This means that she knew the specs
of daughters I carried short,
and I was never alone in their loss.

But, I am the one trimming our line—
the last wooden doll fit into a thimble.

//

I sing off-key and light a candle,
remembering her nightgown

like smoke and how, as she's leaving,
I watch everything ash. A wince split
into every oncoming joy.

My heart squeezes three times.

Vase for the Dead

I wake exhausted,
unable to find
my mother in dreams.

I pick from a jar of river
rocks, suck one,
then sharpen my teeth.

Even cold, my coffee
tastes like rust.
At noon, I lean my head

against a man's chest,
tell him about
javelina that scavenge

our trash in the night.
How they scrub
for seeds and how, last

summer, I planted
a dozen tulips
that were beheaded

by morning. He kisses
me hard, says, *That
should be placed somewhere*

in the body. He means
of a poem. I bite
my lip until it bleeds.

Fall, Hushed Light

You want a story of progress, but it's fall.

I will give you this—I wash the bowls, brush my hair,
clamor about the yard looking for leaves that crochet the light.

What is there to say to loss that is not also a greeting.

Today, the last hibiscus flower withered, snot-yellow,
and the creek bed flooded with weeds.

I do not see the pile under the tree and think about the coming bloom.
I bury them so they will not grow cold, the days shorter now.

There are no more hummingbirds around to pray.
Only ravens—winged funerals sweeping the sky.

My mother said the falling leaves were a crone tucking her children
safe before the snow sheets and turns them blue.

I scrape the plate of uneaten food and bleed—my body dropping
seeds, while foolish men talk of war.

Senescence

My doctor is wearing moccasins—beads, the color of autumn,
sewn onto skin.

She moves soundlessly, skilled, and asks me to take
a deep breath before clearing the y-shaped wire from my body.

It has grown tired, so she is replacing it with another, which means
there is little chance I will become pregnant now, even in dreams.

Before pinching it into place, she asks once more—are you ready?

    //

When I arrive to pick up my youngest from school, another child
is crying. He lifts my glasses to gauge my eyes and decides

that I'm fit, or kind enough, to carry him into quiet, and when he
presses his hair to my chest, I smell a house of books and sour milk,

another woman's kiss at his temples, a song tucked into his sleeves.
We rock and rock the way a birthed body settles into stillness,

and when I do not feel any borders or pangs that this child could never
be mine, I know I am ready to be sealed, the procedure-blood drying,

outside—the dry leaves blushing.

Murmuration

A dream that I sew wings from eyelashes taken off
the dead, pack honey into bones for the long walk.

If someone said, *Live here long enough and your blood*
will mix with the soil, and they meant *your children* and *buried,*

not an honest day's work, you too would flee, flow into this
murmuration to keep safe. How could a country

possibly border its breath? We have already set our tables
for their souls, lit candles for every child fainted

along the path. You are the one counting your steps to nowhere;
they have bodies of water to cross, hunger to outpace.

A dream of safety. Listen, I've seen starlings form mesmerizing
shapes in the sky. But this caravan doesn't need to wow you,

witness. They are you—but, after risking this journey, more human.

Opening My Third Eye to the World

My son's stuffed owl gets ravaged by our dogs,
he wakes me crying because he can hear it in sleep,

a mile away, the real thing, brushing the tips of rye grass
with its hoot all the way to his window, the same grass

we passed and I pointed out the discoloration to mean
the changing into another season. What do I tell him

about this world? What do I let him hold that cannot
be taken? I have stuffed my own mother's memories

into a suitcase too heavy to lift, slipped it under the bed
until I can find the right god to pray, one willing to save us all.

My son climbs into bed next to me, warm with tears,
and unclasps his palm. A single gutted eye falls onto the pillow.

Stocking the Bomb Shelter

I will miss raspberries and unraveled flags
sauntering prayers into the wind.

I will miss stretching my arms to the woman
who sobbed unexpectedly in the school yard,
how she smelled of broth and yarn.

I will miss guilty pleasures I would not swallow,
and miss the never-having.

I will miss puffing dried dandelions, salting
bland hours, lazing in the June sun.

I will miss strangers and the hopeful worlds
creased onto their brows, where they danced
drunk and naked, had the right key to unlock
every painted door.

I will miss jazz and newborn books, steamed linens
and invitations, finding reasons not to attend.

I will miss my son's dervish excitement over rain,
his chapped lips pressing onto the glass.

I tuck my children into bed, and wait out
the hours until their hair smells of dreams.

These too will be paired down to dirt,
the May ash-bloom, the senseless quiet,
the night ticking dead numbers into our heads.

Heavy Metal Morning

When the old man driving his Buick nearly
    cranked into the side of the car where my son sits,

where my son had his hand jutted out to catch
    the smallest meteors that fall and sprinkle our hair like

factory dust, I thought of the hummingbird nest
    abandoned below the branch where it was sewn and how

I tried to wedge an umbrella as awning during
    the sharpest storm, when I could not see yet if the eggs

had chipped and split, or if they were still a hard-
    shell over a heartbeat, as the metal doors and beams

are, and how on the morning news there was a blip
    about a boy whose father slit his throat because he did

not have a babysitter and would not leave him to sleep
    alone, and the news anchor coined it a rash decision.

And now my son is screaming in the backseat, near-impact,
    while all I can hear are tires slipping on gravel and how,

in some twisted way, that father didn't want his child to
    be afraid, and how Styrofoam can feel cold as a knife

because it carries heat away from a hand, which the humming-
    bird must have known because she thought to pack it

between twine and feather-drift, her rash-ruby throat, like
    a spill of gas, a blind-spot until the sun hits just right.

Gifts from the Crows

I leave kitchen scraps & star charts—maps of glass
that broke in the sky.

They slip gifts near my door: paper cups / bright buttons /
bent wire. Tokens so simple I wonder if I've lifted them in sleep.

Barefoot under the gaslights.

    //

I read about houses shored with whale bone & timber washed
up on sand & structured into a stable compound—cement
or stucco. Every woman knows

that even beauty is surrounded by hard.

    //

The most difficult days, I wait to sleep until I hear the metronome
of crows, frenzied by a cast of hawks that screech nearby.

In the morning, crow bones, chewed clean, drop
from the trees.

Their feathers make dark doorways in the snow.

Marrow

It smelled for days before I found the bones, skinned clean
at the base of the drive. I never knew that rot could

sustain, or the precise sharpness of a skunk's teeth, until it died,
when it mattered little. My husband gauges the struggle, decides

whatever took it down was quick. Then, he adds, there are different
degrees of hunger, as if it charts the same course as disease.

We agree the bones in sun are a kind of joy. Exposed. Sometimes
burial is a dusting, sometimes—marrow-deep.

　　　//

My mother has blue days that are blanketed with forgetting—
the horse's feed, how to untangle her hair.

Others, she is sharp with details.

She remembers holding the reins in her hand. How to punch through
leather to cinch. How to hold her palm flat against the sun.

How planes can't take off when the heat is too thin to hold
the wings, their stalled bodies gleaming white on the tarmac.

The air, more dust than breath.

Bleuet

Reading my grandfather's letters home, 1945,
I learn that he saw Madame Butterfly in Paris,

after the war, that there was enough of him left
to feel the rain and realize the lapse since he'd last

laughed. The same day, I read online about a new
color of blue going into a box of crayons. As if

there is a lapse in the tints of sad available
so that our children might draw the world.

Brighter than cobalt, robin's egg,
cerulean, and sky. Bluetiful. I think of the blue

morpho butterfly, its scopic wingspan, flinch-bright,
its underside camouflaged drab, but still nearing

extinct. Oh, America the bluetiful. Why not name the color
thoughts & prayers. A blue not allowed to rest, bright

as in blood before it stains. The cold rain on my grandfather's
face. I used to wonder why the average German man did

nothing to stop such unspeakable horrors. I know now, what
little can be done. So, I will buy this new color for my son

and tell him all is not lost, see—we have given you a way to
fluent tragedy. In your hands, it might morph into something

beautiful, but mostly blue.

Sticks and Stones

My mom-friend complains that her child is saying no too much—
to veggies, to doors, to bedtimes. I say *standard issue.*

She tells me how she hates herself for yelling *all of the time.*
I tell her to put more water into her mouth

to float her anger. Or, if it's an animal clawing—greet it,
do not try to snare it from the haunt of her body, where it dwells.

When mothers give birth, something feral burrows
into that hollow.

> //

My own son wilds, clanks his head. Bashes walls.
He does not know when they are made of glass. He does not feel.

The lifeguard says, *But he looks so normal,* as if she can read auras.
She marks progress by how long she can hold her breath.

I used to breathe for two.

> //

I hold my son in water, spread his arms to float, teach him how to swash
angels in the wake so he'll never be alone.

I add *wide future* to our list of struggles,
and pray I never die.

//

My friend continues to nag—*sibling rivalry, excessive crying, name-calling.* I tell her about the photo of two small boys in Syria.

Foam gunking their lips. How, when you look the heart says *no.*
The brain says *no.* The way their arms are hugged says *no.*

The mother, who is not trained in wailing, says *yes, look*
and lets the animal rise from her throat. She screams until
their names become stone.

Found Objects

I would paint the snow for you
if the street light wouldn't melt it.

I would paint each broken bone kissed
with lip gloss and a tambourine snagging

on a sweater. I would paint the walls as
frozen cities, the shush of traffic, slush

of light, and there would be no *late for
the party* because I would stall fret

and airplane engines from whirling,
the tarmac pigeons still cooing free.

I would paint you. A fingernail moon.
A waxy rind. A bucket of water.

A bombed-out building. The white chalk
of rubble in your hair. A river to wash

in, cool enough that when the swirl licked
your shins, you would feel

your borders blend clean, mix into stone,
grey with breath

but breathing. I would paint the
longest table, and leave the seat
empty, next to yours, room enough

for our elbows to pass and static,
while the wine is being shared
and blissing our mouths into prayer,

a language neither of us speaks,
which is why I would paint us slipped

from our clothes and touching.
Same to same. A raven's feather

swirling about, a basket clogged with
warm bread, loaves halved in crystalline

salt, and when we blink at each other
we see veins that are flowing with blood,

but mostly water. I would paint a placenta-sky,
gamey and wired. Electric.

The wink of a heartbeat
that is mine and not my own,

pulsing like bombs dropping

one, one, one, tearing a hole
in the wall, where a large painting of god

was hung, gold-encrusted,
but now just an opening of light.

I would paint your grave as a pair
of shoes left by the front door,
laces untied and waiting,
toes scuffed, facing out.

Threadbare

There is a sense of progress
after the last wound is sewn—

acorn-eyes tunneled into the doll face,
lips of red thread

curled at the edges to cull dark dreams,
hemp hair twist-swept
into an old rubber band.

The teeth marks repaired—single
stitched, thin reminders of the damage

a mouth can do when hungered
and left alone.

I swat the dog on her nose
although she does not understand

she has done wrong. She wags closer.
I tuck the doll next to my littlest

who might wake to think that sleep
is an erasure of tragedy—

who am I to say that isn't so.
I have been packing the dark

between my ribs with each sharp
edge of hate that grazes this world.

It takes the hours I should be dreaming,
leaves them frayed.

I am no better.

Last night, I paused the needle only
long enough to toss a wasp out

of the screen door
but only after smashing it

with the spine of my favorite book,
morning-wings still crimpled on the floor.

II

Lullaby

Words dull us drowsy,
so we tuck books
into bed.

In one, a herd of elephants
lives under the surface
and holds up

the weight of this world,

when one bows his head,
weary,
we quake.

In another, a catfish swims
beneath the surface

when he thrashes about
the world shakes.

Our stability
is at the mercy
of inhumed hearts.

II.

I trace circles
along my son's back,

the river of nerves
under a ridgeline
of bone,

the smooth
corners that wear memory
down to a science.

I dream
that fish have
no memory,

I dream from what
I've been told,

but catfish can recall
the sound of a human
voice five years
after.

When I hum
this lullaby

it is to calm
the tusks,
the caudal fin,
the myths under
this world that

hold us steady
and let us glimpse

dreams
before
we are rocked
to sleep.

A Closet of Hand-Me-Downs

Again, the house keeps cold. Brown recluse
crawl into my shoes and out of sinks. I mother them away

from my children's beds, blow into my boys' ears
to make certain one spider has not gone rogue and tunneled

that dark. Their bite eats away skin. I seal each spider
in my grandfather's toolbox—the dent-metal he packed lunch

into every day. I sing them hungry while my children
grow out of their clothes and leaves turn the color of lemons,

then tomatoes, long snapped from the vine. I rise
each morning, twirl night-webs into a clear plastic bag, call

them dreams, give my children something to hold
under their pillows, their baby teeth already packed into bullets,

their whistles—shivers in a draft of air.

The Gun Collecting Dust in Our Closet

I loved the world until a man showed me how
easy it is to flick the safety off,

how weighted the end, butted into my shoulder,
the nook where my son burrowed his head to sleep.

Both the bulk of that gun and translucent skin of my son's
forehead stumped my breath. Equally.

What does that say about love?
I imagine mothers who give birth but come home empty,

their breasts leaking anyhow. They loved the world once, too.
Between us, a thin sheet of red. Miles of windows, dark.

And the dust is a lullaby small enough for my hands to fold.
It coats the leaves blanketing the ground.

Stifling wildflowers and weeds. We cannot hold a note
long enough to slow a heart.

To be the first

snow of the long season—

the bough of trees drooped
like my mother's breasts

out of the shower,
she covered them with palms

pressing them close
against skin and ribbed heart,

I was not supposed to know
about the thick tissue of

motherhood
I glanced as shame—

the ground obscured
by layers of leaf-rot

and overgrowth,
that abutment

I explored to escape
but also to know what grew

so close to the house,
which is how my great-grandmother's

ring slipped from my pinkie—
hands too cold, no ting,

that speck of diamond,
an eyelash flutter, stardust.

When I told her, she pushed
me back toward the trees

you best not come home empty-handed—
I scoured, not understanding yet

how a whole history can be stuck
inside of cut and clarity,

instead, a fistful of rabbit poops,
round like dark planets

that showed themselves
so that I would have an offering,

my mother standing by the screen door
the tumor, not yet, but maybe a speck

in her cells,
buried under what, in fall, we had

gushed about being so alive,
so damn beautiful.

Pulp

My husband complains that his promotion
isn't his highest calling. He loses sleep,

paces the night with the kind of anger
that seeds in men.

I dress in a dark closet.
The covered mirror is another

negotiation with my life.
I sweep/scrub/coddle/swat

& call it a lovely morning.
A snip of happy.

I peel a crate of oranges,
rub the rind behind my ears,

against my wrists, rub the heart
against metal tines to flush the juice,

place a follicle on my tongue
until the sweet goes numb.

Breakthrough Bleeding

(Von Willebrand Disease)

My body as malfunction, as smear,
as blood-stacks not tall enough to fall
over each other and mold, the harsh
diagnosis named after a Finnish man,
as in his phrase leaking from my body,
as in scabs are harder to redline into
scars, left unsealed longer, as in I am
an open wound, fragile but not precious,
could die from impact, as in step carefully,
the bruises—small storms along my skin,
as in my mother would hide for days
in shame, as in heredity, as in the inability
to hide where a man gripped her wrist,
rested his weight, as in biting my tongue
could flood my mouth, as in I had to watch
with every nicked kiss to keep from drowning
his voice, as in I learned how to hold poems
soft against gums, tight between my teeth.

Forget-Me-Nots

Today, my mother forgot the word for bathroom
while she was in one. She said, *Dry room, no—wet room, no—*

tell me, then *what are the others called? I'd like to walk them.*

At one point, someone taught me a word I've forgotten.
A room I was already inside. A marriage. A country. A war.

A man's fingers cuffed around my wrist. Someone promised—
it is common, when learning another language, to lose

pieces of your mother tongue. Where the bar lights are also
a call to prayer, and the flowers aching the field are no less

yellow, the spider's bite still poisoned, when I cannot
say their name. My mother will soon lose

my own and even though I understand the way of things,
I will hear the horses, in mourning, nip

at the electric fence, and I will not have the word for shock.

Redress

It's not the spider,

leggy as breath along your cheek,
that wakes you.

It's not the thin yolk of sparrow,

not the hemline pines, the bristled
light, the candle's

drip on sheets gone hard, not
hips brushing

hips as if to sponge a history
of hands wept there,

not *stay* or *promise*,

not the flower picked for
the silver vase,

its yawing bloom,

its absence of wild
once the stem is cut,

but the shirt,
damp on the floor,

that makes

you think *forgiveness,*
and maybe
you are worth saving.

(of use)

I.

The nook
between clavicle and chin

that was a soft lure—

an empty cradle now,
a fled nest.

II.

My hair tines.
It specks with grey.

I fed the color
from my bones

first to one child,
then the next.

III.

My hands in the sugar,
my hands in the dough.

I am here to scrap
the rain

sweet—
to make use
of every drop,

to warm the dish,
clear the plate.

IV.

I dress invisible.

Men glance
shallow,
as if my body
pitted
after birth.

V.

I sigh
and sigh

and the houseplant
takes it all in.

Unfurling

The way you say *guess what*
then nothing after I answer *what*

as if the echo itself
was the only thing desired,

or maybe you are curious about
what loose words might summon between us

after ten years of marriage.

You know, too well, I cannot flick past a good silence
without trying to organize it into herringbone
or hymnody,

so I tell you about each unhappiness
because it's easier to undress.

    //

Before sunrise, you collect handfuls of cicada
skins that cover the trunks of trees
by our door,

arrange them into piles as if there is still song.

When I ask why, you say *guess what, I am afraid of how
you might leave me.*

Their wet, soft bodies unzipped in dark.
Their reasons—transparent.

A Town Praying for Rain

The man at the bar says
the moon isn't full enough
for her milk to drop.

I plug a quarter in
the jukebox and dance
anyway,

the bass beat of slurry
planes bellying low
overhead.

Someone spills a beer
that hints of cinder
at the tail end.

It is in our hair—the ash,
fine coating windows and cars,

the hills—ghost-lit
with loss.

The waitress says
it looks like sunset at noon,

and calls her children
to see if the road
home has closed.

I drive home

by way of grasslands,
past nineteen flags
planted into the earth.

Horses flank the side of the road,
galloping.

For those who cannot haul out
it has come to this—

stamping a name and address
along the body

of the horse
before setting it free.

Salt Ring

I show up at his door.

He knows little about how to embrace me—if it is wrong to hold
and for how long, unsure what happens after time

has been between bodies that once kissed crevices of dark.
What permission the past holds.

He touches my cheek, says *I never regretted you.*
Please, don't make me do that now.

Invites me in. Pours whiskey, neat.
The long hardening of amber.

I find a letter on his desk between stacks of hardcover books.
My letter.

He folded it into a paper airplane, drew rows of passengers
in pencil. They are speechless, grim-lipped.

I say, *There should be flames*, so he knows I am there
as something to be extinguished.

The wings are still intact, he says.
And that is too much hope.

There is mercy in the amount of light that slats between us.
There is mercy in our quiet.

I say, *I loved you.*

He nods, pulls me close and there is a litany of bees
thrumming my spine.

My skin—a season of subtle grey and violets.
His arms—still the shape of waiting.

*I tried. I learned that dahlias grow best in dirt that is tart,
mixed with finely ground bones.*

What else, he asks.

I look at his bed, the untucked sheets.
That has nothing to do with us, he says.

A salt ring around the window,
the tapestry of an ocean exhaling.

Then play for me.

He places the curved body of a guitar
between my legs. Strums.

How to Tell the Memory It Isn't True

Sit it down.

Begin with
how much you love it.

Make it a cup of hibiscus tea,
three cubes of sugar.

Wait for the loose grains
to brush soft as snow

from your palms,
then place both hands

over the heart—
unbutton there

to expose
the weft threads

to show
where the wool

was meant
to slide under,

explain how
the eye can slip,

how the brain

doesn't always hold.
Then wander outside

past the horses
and the gate,

to where the patch
of blanket flowers

are growing by the ditch,
where you've buried

years of yellow notes
and all of your to-dos.

Wait for a hummingbird

to come, to spindle
the loose threads

that you have been pulling
to your chin

and scolding for
not keeping you warm.

Forgive the memory
for being made of feathers,

when you were counting on it
to be firmed as bone.

Before the fevered snow,

there was an eyelet and bright button,

hair snipped from sleeping others
and wed around my finger.

You cut it with your tongue.

And the light that came from your mouth
burned hot, so we didn't need to speak.

I watched instead your chest rise
as if with filament, the stuff of love,
burning us clean.

When an eyelash slipped onto my cheek,
you prayed. A god-wish.

Hallucinating faith.

I left that morning—your fever lifted,
and we woke to April snowfall,
window-fog in bloom.

An unsettled quiet, without the first sounds of breaking.

Just the rye grass bending under my feet,
the dew outstretched on leaves overhead,

the omen of it all.

Please do not let me forget

the first time I looped the bird feeder over the branch
and had to choose which category of seeds
to add in its beaker-thin tube—

Santa Ana, stratus, estuary—
hummingbird, robin, blue jay.

Not hawk. Not raven.

Please do not let me forget the barred wing-feather
that ambled down the drive
before the husk of storm,

a child's hands unable to collapse
around such quick-lightness.

The type of feather that could make a quill, or arrow,
replace the worry-stone that heavies hands,
climbs the latticework of a gale.

A feather that falls from a lack of water
and sways into a pond
is a song—

can be dried and bunched
for sweeping.

Please do not let the quiet dust-handprint
smudge from the surface of wood—
its tiny net, its ghost breath,

knowing too well—
trying to preserve and hold it
all the same.

III

Ylem

The fig's fine seeds. Bees bluster from tree to tree taking each essence
to make a single unit of honey. The magazine says that not wearing
a bra builds muscle, so I droop. We pick antique mason jars, put in
white tea lights, screw them tight, learning how to stay married inside
of *lapse*. In *hiatus*. In the season of white petals that flank the wind,
whist-clusters that smell like cat-piss, spackle the gravel, tiny hoarders
of beauty. Dazed. Seeded. I stand in the drive, globe petals in my hair.
Feeling for walls of glass. Salt in a dip of water. Lit.

Script

He cuts a lime with keys
to keep us awake.

Traffic is slowed due to a slide—
boulders slipping from the face.

The mountain—
a monument to centuries of nonviolent struggle—

is releasing her worries
onto the road.

I try not to admit this as omen.

     //

We find a room off the state route.
Behind—a briar clamped with elk

showing their breath in this cold.

A wandering monk once professed—
breath is the script to your inner state,

his collection basket worth more
than the change nested in it.

     //

My breath catches

at the scrag of hair in the drain—
really a brown recluse
whose bite opens aether.

When I do not find God
in the dresser drawer

to smash the spider into its next
life, I trap it under glass,

then put my pantyhose into
the coffee pot to rinse clean.

My Lover Tells Me How to Use My Hands

A raven *caws* early, stimming on the thinnest
branch. Wings flicker for balance while the man

in my bed thrums on about the faucet *tink*
I haven't yet fixed. My hands—too cold against

his skin, my hands at half-mast, throttled at a dumb-
speed. I think I have done right enough by walking

into this strange house, taking my shoes off at the door,
but when I spread his thighs, he shifts over a litany of pleas—

Cleft. Raze. Furrow. I am learning the language of a body,
how to tend nerve endings and howls that are trenched,

when there is little care to translate my own. After he rises,
I hold my love-line to the window-light, its stammer,

its breakage. But the light is a trick played by a swarm of bees
flickering yellow against the glass, and this line is not love,

just a snag glistening across my palm.

Putin on Horseback

When I told a friend that my mother rode horses, she said, *I'm not that
kind of a person*, the kind who needs to tame something larger
than themselves, to break them. I thought of Putin,

straddled bareback in the sun and what trot must sound like in Russian.
If it is ripened in the mouth for a second before the spittle and push of air.

    //

My father-in-law sleeps in our basement listening to a small radio.
I can hear preachers raising their octaves of faith in Russian.
It pushes through the vents.

When I ask him to translate what they are saying, it is mostly
end-of-days prophesy—God as command, as fury to be released
onto the world.

The kind of fear that tries to break a soul. But for him, it is lullaby,
the dialect of home calming him to sleep.

When the heater kicks in, it covers their voices with a continuous whistle
that sounds like a missile flinging past, never landing.

    //

I study that photo of Putin, the horse gazing at the earth, weary
from the weight of such a man pulling the reins too hard.
But the way its eyes narrow

is anything but broken. The horse has trained himself to see
the slot of light and field between braids of barbed wire.

I am told the dream can only be interpreted by the dreamer,

but my child and I have the same one.

He is drowning. I see him lumped—
a wavy tuft on the bottom.

I ask the nearest man, capable of holding
his breath, to dive in after. Any air I
catch is sharp with rust.

When he emerges, I press on his chest
until a rib cracks

but wake before his lungs can gasp
and heart rhythm.

When he wakes, he thanks me for being
the falcon who broke the surface to grip him,

and also the one
holding space for his return.

He remembers slipping down.

I remember that waiting is
an anticipation of grief.

//

An hour before the light will rise
like an alarm of fur

along morning's spine—he disappears,

comes back into view padding
down the hall,

glancing sidelong at my door,
thanking me for not scratching him
with my talons.

Drought

I stand on the balcony, chunk of granite in my hands—
the snake in the pond below hunts the goldfish

we brought home from the store & named.
Pink Man. Old Pink Man. Shrive. George.

My neighbor shrugs & says, *Everything is starved.*

The ponderosa pine, close to the house & eight stories tall,
gives all of its color to the bark beetles sucking it dry.

I say, *The way of things*—as compass, as white noise, as relief.

The dead tree sways in the dry-storm, rasping our bedroom window.
The needles, drained gold, flicker loose, as if swimming.

It is a form of madness, lightning without rain.
I place the rock in a pile with others, name the snake.

Depression as a Woefully Inadequate Word

I walk the night-neighborhood until I find music and a red
door. I do not have the courage to knock.

Instead, I huddle between trees. Their sweep fattens with dark.
A dark that could swallow me whole

without so much as a yip. I came for the music. For the minor
notes that went tongue to bone, burdened

with their own gravity. The trees know even a beginning
musician can make a heavy metal song

acoustic. It becomes about which instrument is held.
Tonight, it is not a blade, but a single stone,

a spot rubbed soft. Knowing it served its use, that someone
threw it along the side of the road, is a kind of hope.

A violin balancing on a raven's back.

White Coats

We found a stash of nuts and seeds
nestled in the soft hole of bark

just before the first frost cut
the confluence of window-light
and glazed roofs.

The leaves had already sloughed
and crisped, and the birds

on the wire tried to lick the smoke
rising from the house
as if it was an udder.

Please, tell me what wrested that tree
to make it a hollow house
for the wind

and how my body became this bowl
for hands to scrape even the finest crumbs,

and offer them to a bough of blackbirds,
the snow on their oily feathers—newborn
the branch too cold to bend.

Witness

Before the second snow,

my son finds a split of wood
shaped liked a gun—

he loads it with wind
and shoots at a park

bodied with laughter.

    //

A three-year-old girl walks
in front of a swing
in motion,

her mother says,
That is how she will learn.

From impact.

    //

I watch ravens flick
from a loop and scatter,

spreading miles
between their dark bodies.

    //

Only months ago,
my boy carried a wounded

moth to my attention—
a shred in the eyelet pattern—

how willing he was
to hold the breakage
in his hands,

and when he found it
dazed, he lifted

it to the light
and apologized,

as if the one who stumbles
across suffering

carries the same
amount of guilt home.

Tsunami Drills in the High Desert

my child louds
disruptive
gets removed
from the public
library every
reading hour
once a month
hides in a storage
closet active
shooter drills his
teacher with ten
special-needs kids
my son cannot quiet
cranks at the vacuum
and lights too bright
too crowded he tells
me how their bodies
have to stack like Jenga
for the tsunami I cry
at the kitchen table
when he calls it
the best part of his
day we share for
keeps and in the time
it took the noodles
to boil another illogical
prayer was reloaded
to keep our guns safe
keep our anger healthy
enough it burns action

to ash while we dare
to sleep the next day
my son asks to get
dressed for school
in his orange
life vest tells me
you cannot hear the
water coming you're
safe until the wave
pulls back until the
wave reloads

Funeral Details

There will be a hound baying in the distance & the flowers that have just passed their bloom day will slosh in their glass mouths, drunk, & the sermon will grow loud at times, generic as a hot dish brought to grief's door & the collective breath will flinch at *victim, too soon, amen,* which means *all men* & someone will say that the new child's pose is supine in a casket & someone else will try to make it better by saying there's a quick flash of light before a gun goes off & maybe that's what we're all mistaking for heaven.

IV

Eurydice

As a girl, I pretended the sky between slats
was a bed of black widows,

spider silk strung across dark,
the star-bits—their sacs pulsing with eggs.

I was never lonely because I hadn't grown into
any reason to be afraid.

My hair held the silo-stink of dandelion & molded hay.

　　　//

Now, I walk the back alley behind a row of bars, lit,
& the sky is a map of women held under.

I see one beauty walking barefoot down a dirt road,
trying to be soundless. Her hair—wheezing smoke

from the gap of men's mouths. The star is a key jagged
as a knuckle in her hand. She is twenty paces behind,

hoping he doesn't look back.

Nature Prescribed as Remedy

Light moves
in ways I cannot—

over wind chimes,
through the porch lamp,
casting over a wire.

It ghosts the coming cold.
It spills.

        //

My shadow is taut
and leans

over the quiet
hummingbird nest
of thistle-down
and feather-vein,

little leaf-cup
snug on the branch

where the dark
slowed

into a manageable
shape.

There is holy breath
in the wing-flap
of a mother,

in not being able
to touch
the ground.

      //

My dark—
blotted and smeared—

was siphoned
by doctors

who took pens
and prodded the light
to enter.

They held down my tongue,
clipped the stopper.

You will drain now,
they promised.

A clump
of black sadness
tweezed loose.

      //

I have collected this
shoebox of star-matter
and scrap.

When the wind turns
its back, we will pyre
it into a burn

until the smoke
begins to sing
a hymn of ash

and our eyes water,
slipping the constellations
from their prescribed places.

When She Begins to Forget Me

Come winter,
the woodpeckers
are all that is left
but the door opening
startles them into flight.
          This cold
feels skittish without
snow, as if it too could
lift off and flap
over the road.
          The calloused
man at the hardware
store says *unseasonable*
as if his wife slipped bitters
into his tea, where cinnamon
should be.
          Somewhere, we
started giving names to what
does not belong.
          I hear it again
to fill the blank that
flops over my mother's
memories, lays its furred
white over the delicate
frame of her life.
I carry a pound
cake to a neighbor in mourning.
She invites me to sit in the chair
closest to the door.
          She confesses that

when she didn't have enough
sheets, she hung a hand-stitched
rug over the largest mirror.
It spends a week seeing only
its own snags.

Waiting for the Promised Snow

Our marriage therapist slips, says, *This is your eternal struggle—*
one pursues and one withdraws. I think of the emu chasing a man
with half a sandwich across a parking lot. It happened somewhere.
And the man was hungry.

The forecast is hoggish, promising a reckoning—two feet of mountain
snow—but the anchors cannot agree on a start time. When it comes
to being buried alive, the end time feels more consequential.
I would like to know

when the silence that whists between tall pines will lighten. I'm in it
for breadth, for the ravens and crows, the peregrine falcons
that hunt what storms drive into the open.

I've made a stack of sandwiches, wrapped them in foil, left them
on the porch. No one should be running when the stakes are that high,
the ice that hidden and dark. My *I'm sorry,* not enough
salt to clear the road.

My Mother After Brain Surgery

Even drugged, a shunt draining fluid from her brain, the staples
holding the gap where they pried a tumor—the surgeon himself,

made of god particles and skill, the mass splendid because it was
part of her, the mass horrific because it stunted memory and self-care,

even after the anesthesia wore thin and the tubes made her skin
crawl with snakes, she screamed *help mother help*, my grandmother

years dead, when a man reached between her thighs to slip the catheter
free, even when she could not recognize her daughter or name, when

she was helpless and a man's hands were uninvited, causing pain,
she panicked, and when I asked why she was yelling help,

she knew enough to say *that's what we have to do, isn't it?*

This View

did not predict depression
did not account for barefoot over broken glass
did not count the cutlery, hide the knives
did not install the top latch or
forget to leave night-shoes by the door, for wandering
did not fold notes into the wood-pecked holes
did not bunch stray feathers between rocks
did not trample the grass, or bust lips
did not slip the reflection from the splintered frame
did not pretend to know, unflinchingly, the source of this howl

Turning into Another Year

This year will be better. We will study the wood frog that comes
back to life after a long freeze—as curiosity, not metaphor.

I will sage the corners of my mouth and learn to tolerate
the texture of popsicle sticks.

I will depress my breath long enough to wave at the other mothers
in the drop-off line—without cursing, without crossing myself as elegy.

This year will be filled with forgetting, which is gutting—
her struggle to summon my name when I unknot her hair,

stitch her coffee with cream. What existed in her blood months
before I was born.

I will practice motherlessness. Which cannot be perfected
because of memory—mine.

I will practice making my children shatterproof.
I have been given no other choice.

I will teach my son how to read cursive as our breath
in the still-cold morning.

I will go hunting with a fist of feathers and show my unchecked
skin to the teeth of something feral,

a black bear or mountain lion, my softest parts reddened by sun,
marked as mistake, or deliciously rare.

A Thousand Words Are Worth a Picture

I cull them—scattered in the hay bales, in the trough,
swished into the mare's tail like sun,

put them in a mason jar by the window, so, when
the time comes, you'll have something to pick from

to name the girl buttoning your shirt, wiping your cheek.
I will not mind *canter, reins, paddock.*

There were years of you where I never had a name
anyhow. The difference—the photo that sits on the sill

will soon lose its nowness, but I will never live a year
without you tacked under my tongue.

Mother, you have always been mine to carry.

So, please, when you are tired, you can whisper *fetlock,*
cinch, wean, and I'll know how to tuck you in.

We'll pretend that your hair is still
that stream of dark and all the boys have formed

a line, waiting to hold your hand into the next dance.

Close

A moth swats the light with coffered wings.

My mother wraps her bones in blankets—
there is little between us now, not padded flesh, not memory.

She is weightless. I draw her likeness in mud in front of the barn door
with salt & watch ants carry flecks to the base of the mountain.
Her dreams. Her needs.

I pinch what's left & hide it in my pocket.

She stands in a nightgown I've picked, but cannot unlock the buttons.
There must be more than reliance after we are chewed to the core.

She apologizes for being a mother-burden, for the water being too hot
when I unwind the rivers from her hands to prove there is still
some part that floats.

The doctors promise we are close to a cure.
Come dark, we try to catch the moon in a bucket of water.

Overwhelmed

The red ball slipped into the pond we haven't cleaned in seasons,
the way I submerge the alarm under sleep, bleep happiness, as an act
to remember doing, as almost empty. I can run on fumes. I brag to the
doctor/mechanic/mother picking her child up at school who says she
could park her car in the dark circling my eyes. I could conceal, but
callery pears are blooming so white over all the empty lots and smell
like piss. Invasive. I carry emergency numbers in my pocket that brood.
I've grown full. I don't remember promising to stitch the lapse in this
world, offering to carry the water. But here I am, afraid my hands are
the sliver chipped into the painted cup. Indigo. Bone.

Difference

The monsoons arrive like scissors
pointing down—what's the difference,
really, when she takes them with her
hands, opens their mouths and tries
to cut the whites of her nails.

                            The garden
bed bleeds—tulip mouths open
red for a parade of dark feathers.
Bark beetles thrive in the bellies
of pines. We say *renewing the forest*,
and *outbreak*, until they overtake
the one closest to our house, then,
loud from open windows, we begin
to use the word *death*.

Poem on My Mother's Birthday
(Three Days After Her Death)

They have not burned your body yet. This thought
alone is noxious enough to keep me from any blue

hour of sleep. I have seen the morgue trays like silver
toboggans at the base of a hill. All joy behind.

Do you remember the holiday last, when I knit a scarf
that curved like a hug. It was all accident.

All numb thumbs. I want to wrap you in it now. Brush
what's left of your hair back to dark. But I can't.

So, I start your day with song—dress my children thick
for the world outside, cover their mouths, let their

breath soak through, then park the car where you
are kept and wait for black smoke to rise. A candle-wish.

And when the weather turns, I'll try to slip you from
the thread-work of snow—all melt-soft and fuzzed. All wrong.

Freeing My Hands

He says happiness
is comprised of equal parts gratitude and joy—

the ribbon tied to the fence for no reason
other than to float and be tethered at the same time—

and that maybe, each yap is a coyote calling out to hunger as celebration:
a lightening, not a cramp.

He takes the sad song I've been patching, folds it against the seam,
gives me the last cup, rim smudged red as my mother's laugh.

I drink it in, spend the morning plucking the guitar despite a broken string.
Its hallelujah—a feather-drift. A wingspan.

//

By afternoon, there's a man grinding wood stumps beneath my window,
shavings spraying like confetti.

He says, *Your one wild and precious life*—
and I float

away from bone, into soft tissue, into water.

Jasmine

The instructor chooses a pink square,
numbs his hands enough for us to follow,
speaks the language of folds—
mountains and valleys.

This is my therapy,
salvaging a room of scraps
that bend.

Graceful as blood-cuts
lining my fingertips
from grasping too quickly.

Today, I choose a pale, unwanted piece—
pre-creased—another's failed attempt
at nestling the lip against the line.

He explains, a single sheet makes both—
mother and child, is alimental,
unfettered.

To ensure it doesn't drift too far,
we secure it with a clip.

But first, we collapse and hush
layers to make newborn creases,

joke about how a cup
of water could be our undoing

and I'm there, as quickly as she's not—
her glass by the bedside table,
I could not bear to move,

dingy ring, the color of jasmine,
then straw—
a single, dried smear.

Tomorrow, he promises,
we will add a star-shaped
flower to her hair.

The World in Which I Open Google Earth and My Mother Is Feeding the Horses

I imagined it differently. The paddock flooded.
The donkey and sheep, a fence over, cuddled
under the mare. I want to pull up and show
her my new haircut so she can make that face,
then make the word *okay* sound like a derailment.
I want to tell her about the fire and how our
neighbor scrambled the yard gathering her chickens
through smoke. I never found out what she did
with them, if she scrunched those warm feathery
bodies into the back of her station wagon and took
off for Tempe, or Tallahassee. My mother would
know. She wanted to become the patron saint of
animals and I imagine she hasn't stopped auditioning
for the gig. I imagined that she would come to me, too,
after death. After whiskey, or fucking on a Tuesday
morning, when the kids were in school and the ravens
etched treetop to treetop, hunting. After crying when
her sick-bed blanket made it into my hands. After her
guitar string broke, or the prayer to some Sunday-
school saint hedges out of my mouth. The one where
I am in the drop-off line and wince handing my children
over. I ask her to stay with them, keep them alive.
In her eyes, I was always coming up short, why not
turn the reins over now that she is ephemera. But,
it turns out, she has been home all along, arranging
the horses' feed bags the exact way they like them. As if
she knew that would be the one thing we would never
figure out alone.

Elegy

Her horses have shed their coats—they dream
of bones rising under the fevered snow.

Flyaway hairs float into a stream of light
like dust, or skin cells, like touch

Notes

"Your one wild and precious life" is from Mary Oliver's poem "The Summer Day."
"Jasmine" was the name of my mother's favorite horse.

Acknowledgments

I am grateful to the editors of the following publications who first published versions of these poems:

3Elements Review	"Gifts from the Crows"
Black Fox Literary Magazine	"Come Winter"
Breakwater Review	"Forget-Me-Nots"
Cahoodaloodaling	"(of use)"
Cliterature	"Senescence"
COG Literary Journal	"Found Objects," "Lullaby"
The Comstock Review	"Before the Fevered Snow," "Redress"
Corpore Sano Anthology	"Breakthrough Bleeding"
ELM	"How to Tell the Memory It Isn't True"
Glass: A Journal of Poetry	"Drought"
Heavy Feather Review	"The World in Which I Open Google Earth and My Mother Is Feeding the Horses"
Juxtaprose	"Witness"
Light Journal	"Vase for the Dead"
Minerva Rising	"When She Begins to Forget Me," "Boneyard"
The MOON Magazine	"I Will Explain"
Nimrod International Journal	"A Thousand Words Are Worth a Picture," "Eurydice," "Marrow," "Pulp," "Unfurling"
Panoplyzine	"My Lover Tells Me How to Use My Hands"
Poets Reading the News	"Another Word," "Bleuet," "Dropped Stitch," "Funeral Details," "Murmuration," "Putin on Horseback"
Rattle	"A Town Praying for Rain"
San Pedro River Review	"Depression as a Woefully Inadequate Word"

Smartish Pace	"Opening My Third Eye to the World"
Topic Journal	"Overwhelmed"
Varnish	"Threadbare"

"A Thousand Words Are Worth a Picture," "Eurydice," "Marrow," "Pulp," and "Unfurling" were awarded Second Prize in the Pablo Neruda Prize for Poetry.

"Opening My Third Eye to the World" won the 2018 Beullah Rose Poetry Prize.

"Found Objects" and "Lullaby" won the 2017 COG Poetry Award.

"Forget-Me-Nots" was named Honorable Mention in the Peseroff Prize Poetry Contest.

"White Coats" was originally published in the chapbook *Unspeakable Light* by Throwback Books.

Megan Merchant holds an MFA degree in International Creative Writing from UNLV and is the author of three full-length poetry collections: *Gravel Ghosts* (2016), *The Dark's Humming* (2015 Lyrebird Award Winner, 2017), *Grief Flowers* (2018), four chapbooks, and a children's book, *These Words I Shaped for You* (Philomel Books/Penguin Random House). She was awarded the 2016-2017 COG Literary Award, the 2018 Beullah Rose Poetry Prize, and most recently, second place in the Pablo Neruda Prize for Poetry. She is an editor at *Pirene's Fountain* and *The Comstock Review*. Merchant lives in Prescott, AZ with her husband and two children. You can find her work at meganmerchant.wix.com/poet.

A NOTE ON THE TYPE

The titles in this book are set in Bembo, a typeface
created by the Monotype corporation in 1928 to
mimic the type used in 15th and 16th century Italian
printmakers' work. The body text of this book is set
using Bell, a typeface originally cut in the late 18th
century for the British Letter Foundry whose operator,
John Bell, serves as its namesake.

This book would not have been possible
without the hard work of our staff.

We would like to acknowledge:

TOMMY SHEFFIELD *Managing Editor*
ROSE STRODE *Assistant Editor*
MEGHAN McNAMARA *Media & Marketing Advisor*

STILL
HOUSE
PRESS

CPSIA information can be obtained
at www.ICGtesting.com
Printed in the USA
FSHW011605180120
66240FS